The Grasshopper and the Ants

Written by Pippa Goodhart

Illustrated by Juanbjuan Oliver

Collins

T0337555

It was spring. Grasshopper lifted her violin to her shoulder and began to play.

"The ants are sowing seeds.
Sun will shine and it will pour with rain,
to make the seeds grow into grain,"
sang Grasshopper.

3

Summer arrived.

"The ants all hoe
to help the grain grow," sang Grasshopper.

The crop grew tall.

Grasshopper played and sang, "The ants harvest the golden grain as I sing and play a tune on my violin."

"There! Lots of golden grain to share," said Big Ant. The ants started to chew.

8

"Can I eat some too?" asked Grasshopper.

9

"No!" said Big Ant. "You didn't work to grow it, so you can't have it. That's fair."

Little Ant told Grasshopper, "There is a time to work and a time to play. You played as we worked."

"That makes me sad," responded Grasshopper.
"It would be good to share."

Winter came. It was cold.

The group of ants munched all the grain.
But they were discontented.

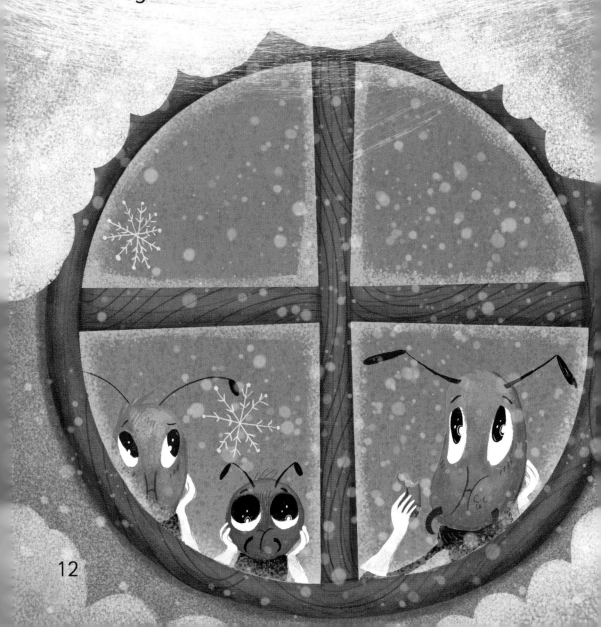

Grasshopper sang songs, but wished she had some grain to eat.

"I miss Grasshopper's music," sighed Big Ant.
"I miss Grasshopper," said Little Ant.

14

"Come to our home and share our grain," said the ants.

It would be wonderful if you would play your violin.

16

Grasshopper played her violin and sang.
The ants skipped about.

19

There are times to work and times to play ...

but it is always good to share.

What works best?

After reading

Letters and Sounds: Phase 5

Word count: 250

Focus phonemes: /ai/ ay, ey, a-e /ee/ ea /igh/ i-e, i /oa/ ow, o, oe, ou, o-e /oo/ ew, u-e, ou, u /oo/ oul /ow/ ou /u/ o, o-e /or/ our, al /ur/ or /ar/ a /air/ ere, are /o/ a

Common exception words: to, the, are, into, my, of, said, have, little, we, me, were, she, our, what, be

Curriculum links: Animals, including humans; PSHE

National Curriculum learning objectives: Reading/word reading: read other words of more than one syllable that contain taught GPCs; Reading/comprehension: understand both the books they can already read accurately and fluently and those they listen to by checking that the text makes sense to them as they read, and correcting inaccurate reading; become very familiar with key stories, fairy stories and traditional tales, retelling them and considering their particular characteristics

Developing fluency

- Your child may enjoy hearing you read the book.
- You could each choose the part of one character in the story and read it with expression.

Phonic practice

- Read page 5 to your child. Ask:
  - Can you find two words that rhyme? (*hoe, grow*)
  - For each word, can you point to the part of the word that represents the /oa/ sound? (*oe, ow*)
  - Can you think of other words that contain the /oa/ sound? (e.g. *toad, low*)
- You could now do the same with the /ai/ sound on page 7. (*play, grain*)

Extending vocabulary

- Ask your child if they can think of an antonym (opposite) for each of the following words:

  grew (e.g. *shrank*)

  sad (e.g. *happy*)

  arrived (e.g. *left*)

  started (e.g. *stopped*)

  responded (e.g. *ignored*)